Alex Rodriguez

by Kim Covert

Reading Consultant:
Dr. Robert Miller
Professor of Special Education
Minnesota State University, Mankato

CAPSTONE
HIGH-INTEREST
BOOKS

an imprint of Capstone Press
Mankato, Minnesota

Capstone High-Interest Books are published by Capstone Press
151 Good Counsel Drive, P.O. Box 669, Mankato, Minnesota 56002
http://www.capstone-press.com

Library of Congress Cataloging-in-Publication Data
Covert, Kim.
    Alex Rodriguez/by Kim Covert.
    p. cm.—(Sports heroes)
    Includes bibliographical references and index.
    Summary: Traces the life and baseball career of Texas Ranger shortstop
Alex Rodriguez.
    ISBN 0-7368-1051-X
    1. Rodriguez, Alex, 1975– —Juvenile literature. 2. Baseball players—United
States—Biography—Juvenile literature. [1. Rodriguez, Alex, 1975– 2. Baseball
players. 3. Dominican Americans—Biography.] I. Title. II. Sports heroes (Mankato,
Minn.)
GV865.R62 C68 2002
796.357'092—dc21   2001003636

Editorial Credits
Matt Doeden, editor; Timothy Halldin, cover and interior designer; Katy Kudela,
    photo researcher

Photo Credits
ALLSPORT PHOTOGRAPHY/Jonathan Daniel, cover, 25; Al Bello, 4; Scott Halleran,
    7, 38; M. David Leeds, 8; Ronald Martinez, 10, 42; Ezra Shaw, 12; Jim Commentucci,
    21; Stephan Dunn, 26; Otto Greule, 29, 37
AP/Wide World Photos/Jeffrey Boan, 14; Marta Lavandier, 17
SportsChrome-USA/Vincent Manniello, 18, 23; Rob Tringali Jr., 30, 33, 34
Tom DiPace, 41

1 2 3 4 5 6 07 06 05 04 03 02

Table of Contents

CHAPTER 1

The 40-40 Club

On September 5, 1998, the Seattle Mariners were playing the Baltimore Orioles. Seattle shortstop Alex Rodriguez hit a single in the fifth inning. He stood on first base as Seattle outfielder Ken Griffey Jr. stepped to the plate.

Alex took a lead off first base. He took off to second on the second pitch to Griffey. Alex slid and held the base. It was his 40th stolen base of the year.

Two weeks later, the Mariners played the Anaheim Angels. Alex stepped up to bat in the first inning. Jack McDowell was the Angels' pitcher. McDowell threw a high fastball. Alex drove it 390 feet (119 meters) into the front row

In 1998, Alex stole 46 bases and hit 42 home runs.

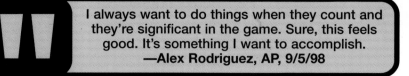

of the bleachers on the right side of center field. It was his 40th home run of the year.

Alex had joined the 40-40 club. He stole 40 bases and hit 40 home runs in one season. Only Barry Bonds and Jose Canseco had accomplished this feat before him. Alex ended the 1998 season with 42 home runs and 46 stolen bases.

About Alex Rodriguez

Alex Rodriguez is an All-Star shortstop. He began his career in 1994 with the Seattle Mariners. He now plays for the Texas Rangers. Alex's fans often call him "A-Rod."

Many baseball experts believe that Alex is the best shortstop in baseball today. Some experts believe that he is the most complete player in baseball. He hits for power and for a good average. He runs fast. He also is a good fielder.

On December 11, 2000, Alex became the highest paid player in team sports. He signed a 10-year contract with the Rangers for $252 million. Alex was only 25 years old when he signed the contract.

Alex Rodriguez

Major League Batting Statistics

Year	Team	Games	Hits	HR	RBI	SB	AVG
1994	SEA	17	11	0	2	3	.204
1995	SEA	48	33	5	19	4	.232
1996	SEA	146	215	36	123	15	.358
1997	SEA	141	176	23	84	29	.300
1998	SEA	161	213	42	124	46	.310
1999	SEA	129	143	42	111	21	.285
2000	SEA	148	175	41	132	15	.316
2001	TEX	162	201	52	135	18	.318
Career		952	1,167	241	730	151	.311

CHAPTER 2

The Early Years

Alex Rodriguez was born July 27, 1975, in New York City. He is the youngest child of Victor and Lourdes Rodriguez. Victor worked in the family's shoe store. Lourdes worked at an automobile factory. Alex has an older brother named Joe and an older sister named Susy.

The family moved to the Dominican Republic when Alex was 4. Many of Alex's relatives lived there. Victor had played baseball in the Dominican Republic when he was young. He taught Alex how to swing a bat. He and Alex often played catch. Alex also played sports after school with neighborhood friends.

Alex was born July 27, 1975.

Alex always has enjoyed playing baseball.

Difficult Times

In 1983, the Dominican Republic's economy was not strong. Alex's family could not make enough money to stay there. When Alex was 8, the Rodriguez family had to sell their home. They moved to Miami, Florida.

Alex attended Everglades Elementary School in Miami. At first, school was difficult for him. Alex spoke only Spanish. It took him two years to learn English.

When Alex was 9, Victor left his family to find work in New York City. Alex was certain that he would come back. But Victor never returned.

After Victor left, the family struggled to earn enough money. Lourdes worked at two restaurants as a waitress. Joe and Susy also had jobs to help pay the bills.

Boys Club

Alex's best friend was J. D. Arteaga. The two boys often played together. They enjoyed playing sports. Juan Diego Arteaga was J. D.'s father. Juan suggested that Alex join the Boys Club of Miami. This club had many activities for children and teenagers. It also had the best youth baseball teams in the city.

Juan was kind to Alex. He helped pay for his baseball fees. He bought him gloves, spikes, and other equipment. He drove Alex

A HERO'S HERO

Cal Ripken Jr.

Alex watched many baseball players as he grew up. Cal Ripken Jr. was Alex's favorite baseball hero. Alex hung a poster of Ripken in his room. He also named his dog "Ripper."

Ripken began his career in 1982 as a shortstop for the Baltimore Orioles. He also played third base later in his career. Ripken was the American League's Most Valuable Player in 1983 and 1991. He also played in 19 All-Star Games during his career. Ripken's last season in the majors was 2001.

Ripken holds the major league record for playing in the most consecutive games. He played in 2,632 games in a row from 1982 to 1998.

and J. D. to their games. He made sure that Alex did not go home to an empty house. Juan helped take the place of Alex's missing father.

Alex became a star player for his Boys Club baseball team. He played shortstop. Alex won the league batting title in his first year on the team. He helped his team win the city championship three times.

Eddy Rodriguez coached the team. In the summer, Eddy often made the team practice twice each day. He taught Alex the importance of hard work and practice.

Eddy had played minor league baseball. He had coached many professional players when they were young. He told Alex stories about these players. These stories made Alex think about becoming a professional baseball player.

High School

Alex attended Westminster Christian High School in Miami. He studied hard and earned good grades. He played football, basketball, and baseball.

In 12th grade, Alex won the Gatorade Award as Florida's top student-athlete.

Alex played starting shortstop on the baseball team in 10th grade. He was a good fielder. But his batting average was only .256.

Rich Hofman was Westminster's baseball coach. Hofman had helped 29 high school players advance to professional baseball. Hofman believed that Alex would play major league baseball someday. He told Alex to keep practicing.

Alex worked hard the summer after 10th grade. He lifted weights and practiced hitting. By 11th grade, he could bench-press 310 pounds (141 kilograms). He could hit the ball 400 feet (122 meters).

In the fall of 1991, Alex was the starting quarterback on the football team. He earned All-State honors and set many passing records for the school. He led the team to a 9-1 record.

Alex also was a star player on the baseball team. He helped the team finish with a 33-2 record. Alex ended the season with a .477 batting average. He scored 52 runs and stole 42 bases. The National High School Coaches Association and *Baseball America* magazine named Westminster the national champions.

That summer, Alex played on the U.S. National Junior Team. He hit .425. Alex helped lead the team to a second-place finish at the 1992 World Junior Championships in Mexico.

The Draft

Alex had another excellent baseball season in 12th grade. He batted .505 and had nine home runs, 36 RBIs, and 35 stolen bases. He was named the *USA Baseball* Junior Player of the Year. He also earned the Gatorade Award. This honor is given to each state's top high school student-athlete. Winners of the award must be both top athletes and top students.

Alex was the best-known high school baseball player in the country. There were 68 major league scouts at Westminster's opening game. The scouts were deciding whether major league teams should draft Alex. Six of the scouts worked for the Seattle Mariners. Seattle had the first pick in the June draft.

On June 3, 1993, the Mariners selected Alex with the first pick. Alex chose Scott Boras as his agent. Boras's job was to work out a contract between Alex and the Mariners. Boras and the Mariners did not agree on Alex's salary. They argued about the contract throughout the summer.

That summer, Alex enrolled at the University of Miami. He planned to attend college there if he did not join the Mariners.

On June 3, the Mariners called Alex to tell him they had selected him in the draft.

On August 30, the Mariners offered Alex a three-year contract for $1.3 million. He accepted their offer. He flew to Seattle a few days after signing a contract with the Mariners. He talked to Ken Griffey Jr. about playing for Seattle. Griffey was the Mariners' star player. He helped Alex look forward to his professional baseball career.

CHAPTER 3

Minor Leagues

In 1994, Alex attended his first spring training camp. He saw how hard professional baseball players worked. Alex learned by watching the experienced players.

Alex began the season in the minor leagues. He played for the Appleton Foxes in Appleton, Wisconsin. The Foxes were the Mariners' Class A team in the Midwest League. Carlos Lezcano managed the Foxes. Lezcano noticed that Alex learned quickly and had many skills. Alex batted .319 in 65 games with the Foxes.

Alex began his professional baseball career in 1994.

On June 16, the Mariners moved Alex up to the Jacksonville Suns in the Class AA Southern League. He hit a home run in his first at-bat with the team.

First Major League Games

On July 7, 1994, the Mariners asked Alex to join the team in Boston, Massachusetts. They were playing the Boston Red Sox.

On July 8, Alex played in his first major league game. He was the starting shortstop. Alex was very nervous. He was only 18 years old. He was the youngest player to play in the major leagues in 10 years. Lourdes was in the stands to watch her son play. Alex did not have any hits in his first game. But he played well in the field.

The Mariners played the Red Sox again the next night. Alex had two hits and stole a base. He also made a good defensive play. He dove toward third base to catch a ball headed for the outfield. Alex put the runner out with a strong throw to first base.

Alex played his first major league game at Fenway Park in Boston.

Back to the Minors

Alex had trouble in the major leagues. He did not hit well. He often swung at bad pitches. On August 2, the Mariners sent Alex back to the minor leagues.

Alex finished the season in Calgary, Alberta, Canada. He played for the Class AAA Calgary Cannons in the Pacific Coast League. He hit .311 in 32 games. He had six home runs, 21 RBIs, and two stolen bases.

Alex played in all four professional baseball levels during the 1994 season. He was named Seattle's Minor League Player of the Year and the Midwest League's Prospect of the Year.

That winter, the Mariners sent Alex to play in the Dominican Republic. Alex improved while playing in the winter league. Alex worked on being more selective at the plate. He learned which pitches he should not try to hit.

Last Minor League Season

Alex started the 1995 season in Tacoma, Washington. He played with the Tacoma

Alex played in all four levels of professional baseball in 1994.

Rainiers. This team was the Mariners' new Class AAA team. Alex hit very well with Tacoma. He had a .360 batting average in his 54 games with the team. He hit 15 home runs and 45 RBIs. He was named Most Exciting Player of the Pacific Coast League.

The Mariners often moved players back and forth from Tacoma to Seattle. The team brought Alex to Seattle three times. He did not hit well with the Mariners. His average was in the low .200s. The team sent him back to play with the Rainiers each time.

Alex was unhappy after being sent back the third time. He called Lourdes. He told her that he hated baseball and wanted to quit. Lourdes encouraged her son to keep working on his skills. She told him that she knew he was going to succeed.

Alex listened to his mother. He wanted to prove that he belonged in the majors. He rejoined the Mariners for the fourth time on August 31. This time, the team did not send him back to the minor leagues.

Alex joined the Mariners for good near the end of the 1995 season.

CHAPTER 4

The Majors

Alex worked hard during spring training in 1996. He and second baseman Joey Cora practiced double plays early each morning. Alex asked his teammate Edgar Martinez for advice on hitting the ball. Martinez was the 1995 American League batting champion. Alex also worked with Seattle batting coach Lee Elia to improve his swing.

Alex's hard work paid off. Seattle Mariners manager Lou Piniella gave Alex the starting shortstop position. In May, Piniella placed Alex second in the batting lineup. Some baseball experts thought that Alex was too

Alex became the Mariners' starting shortstop in 1996.

young and inexperienced to bat second in the lineup. But Alex showed everyone that he could handle the challenge.

Batting Champion

The Mariners began the 1996 season against the Chicago White Sox. The game lasted 12 innings. In the final inning, the bases were loaded. The score was tied 2-2. Alex came up to bat. He hit a single that drove in the winning run.

Alex went on to have an outstanding season in 1996. His .358 batting average was the best in the major leagues. It was the third highest average ever hit by a shortstop.

Alex set five major league records for a shortstop. He had 215 hits, 54 doubles, 141 runs, 91 extra-base hits, and a .631 slugging percentage. He also played good defense. He made only 15 errors in the field.

Alex also earned other honors. He played in his first All-Star Game. He was the youngest shortstop ever to play in an All-Star Game. He

Alex's .358 batting average was the highest in the major leagues in 1996.

also won his first Silver Slugger Award. This award goes to the best major league hitters at each position. *The Sporting News* and the Associated Press named Alex Player of the Year. He finished second in the American League MVP voting. The Rangers' Juan Gonzalez won the award.

In July 1996, Alex signed a new contract with the Mariners. He agreed to play with the team for four more years.

Hitting for the Cycle

On June 5, 1997, the Mariners played the Detroit Tigers. Alex hit a home run in the first inning. He hit a single to right field in the fourth inning. He then hit a long drive to center field for a triple in the eighth inning.

Alex needed only a double to hit for the cycle. In the ninth inning, Alex hit a ball down the right-field line. He slowed down as he approached first base. First base coach Sam Majias told him to keep going. Alex reached

Alex's speed, power, and fielding ability quickly made him one of baseball's biggest stars.

second base safely. He was the second player in the Mariners' history to hit for the cycle.

Alex's performance helped the Mariners win the game. They went on to win the American League West division. But they lost to the Baltimore Orioles in the playoffs.

Losing Seasons

Alex worked hard after the 1997 season to improve his fitness. He ran and lifted weights. He was much stronger in 1998. He ran faster and hit with more power. Alex led the American League in hits. He was voted as starting shortstop on the American League All-Star team. He also won his second Silver Slugger Award.

The Mariners did not have a successful season in 1998. They finished the season 76-85. They did not advance to the playoffs.

Alex started in only 129 games during the 1999 season. On April 7, he went on the disabled list. He had surgery to repair an injury to his left knee. He did not play for five weeks.

Alex started in only 129 games during the 1999 season.

Alex returned to play on May 14. The Mariners were playing the Kansas City Royals at the Seattle Kingdome. Alex hit a home run in his first at-bat. He also stole a base.

Alex ended the season with a .285 batting average. He hit 42 home runs and stole 21 bases. But the Mariners finished the season 79-83. They did not reach the playoffs.

CHAPTER 5

Alex Rodriguez Today

Alex played very well during the 2000 season. He had no errors in 50 games from May 14 to July 7. He was selected to play in his fourth All-Star Game. But he could not play in it because of a knee injury.

In June, Alex decided to meet with his father. It was the first time Alex had seen Victor since Victor had left the family. Alex and Victor both were nervous to see each other. They greeted each other with a big hug. Alex still could not understand why his father

---

Alex went 50 straight games without an error in 2000.

left his family. But Alex had learned to forgive him.

Reaching the Playoffs

In September 2000, Alex was in a hitting slump. He had only three hits in 29 at-bats. On September 30, the Mariners were playing the Anaheim Angels. Seattle needed to win the game to have a chance of reaching the playoffs.

Alex hit a two-run home run in the first inning. He drove home a run in the fourth inning with a single. Alex then slammed a three-run home run in the sixth inning. It was his 40th home run of the season. He hit a sacrifice fly in the ninth. This run gave Alex seven RBIs. He tied his career high for RBIs in a single game. The Mariners defeated the Angels 21-9.

The Mariners went on to defeat the Chicago White Sox in the first round of the playoffs. They faced the New York Yankees in the American League Championship Series (ALCS). The winner would play in the World Series.

Alex led the Mariners to a playoff series win against the White Sox in 2000.

Alex signed a $252 million contract to join the Rangers.

On October 17, the Mariners lost to New York in the sixth game of the ALCS. It was Alex's last game as a Mariner.

A Texas Ranger

Alex was a free agent after the 2000 season. He could choose to sign a contract with any major league team. Mariner fans wanted Alex to stay in Seattle. But many other teams wanted to sign Alex.

Alex decided to play for the Texas Rangers. The Rangers had never played beyond the first round of the playoffs. Tom Hicks is the owner of the Rangers. Hicks said that he wanted Alex to help the team win the World Series.

On May 12, 2001, Alex and the Rangers played the Chicago White Sox. Alex entered the game with 199 career home runs. In the second inning, Alex hit a two-run home run. He became the fifth-youngest player to hit 200 career home runs. In the ninth inning, Alex hit another home run. He ended the game with six RBIs. But Alex's effort was not enough. The White Sox won the game 12-11.

In 2001, Cal Ripken Jr. announced that he would retire at the end of the season. Baseball fans elected him to play third base for the American League All-Star team. The fans elected Alex to play shortstop. Alex wanted Ripken to start the game at shortstop. Alex had grown up watching Ripken play shortstop. In the first inning, Alex told Ripken to switch positions with him. Ripken played the first inning of his final All-Star Game as the shortstop. Alex played third base.

Texas did not have a successful 2001 season. But Alex played very well. He batted .318. His 52 home runs were the most by a shortstop in baseball history.

Working for Children

Alex works with many groups that help children. He hosts an annual dinner to raise money for the Boys and Girls Clubs of Miami. He donated money to help rebuild the Miami Boys Club baseball field. Alex also started a scholarship fund at Westminster Christian High School. The fund helps students pay for college. Alex even wrote a children's book titled *Hit a Grand Slam!*

In 1996, Alex started the Grand Slam for Kids program in Seattle. This program encourages students to do well in reading, math, physical fitness, and citizenship. Alex often speaks at schools to tell children about the importance of education.

Alex often spends time with children. He teaches them about setting goals in their lives.

Career Highlights

1975—Alex is born July 27 in New York City.

1993—Alex is named the *USA Baseball* Junior Player of the Year and wins the Gatorade Award; the Mariners choose Alex with the first overall pick in the draft.

1994—On July 8, Alex plays in his first major league game for the Mariners.

1995—Alex is named the Pacific Coast League's Most Exciting Player.

1996—Alex plays in his first All-Star Game; he leads the major leagues with a .358 average; *The Sporting News* and the Associated Press name Alex the Player of the Year.

1997—Alex becomes the second player in Mariners history to hit for the cycle; fans elect Alex to be the starting shortstop in the All-Star Game.

1998—Alex becomes the third player in baseball history to join the 40-40 club; he sets the American League record for shortstops with 42 home runs in a season.

2000—In December, Alex signs a 10-year, $252-million contract with the Texas Rangers; the contract makes Alex the highest paid player in team sports.

2001—Alex becomes the fifth-youngest player to hit 200 career home runs; his 52 home runs of the season set a major league record for a shortstop.

Words to Know

contract (KON-trakt)—an agreement between an owner and a player; contracts determine players' salaries.

donate (DOH-nate)—to give something as a gift

free agent (FREE AY-juhnt)—a player who is free to sign with any team

professional (pruh-FESH-uh-nuhl)—an athlete who is paid to participate in a sport

scholarship (SKOL-ur-ship)—a grant of money that helps a student pay for education costs

To Learn More

Rodriguez, Alex, and Greg Brown. *Hit a Grand Slam!* Dallas: Taylor Publishing, 1998.

Stewart, Mark. *Alex Rodriguez: Gunning for Greatness.* Baseball's New Wave. Brookfield, Conn.: Millbrook Press, 1999.

Thornley, Stew. *Alex Rodriguez: Slugging Shortstop.* Sports Achievers Biographies. Minneapolis: Lerner Publications, 1998.

Useful Addresses

Major League Baseball
Office of the Commissioner of Baseball
245 Park Avenue
31st floor
New York, NY 10167

National Baseball Hall of Fame and Museum
P.O. Box 590
Cooperstown, NY 13326

Texas Rangers
1000 Ballpark Way
Arlington, TX 76011

Internet Sites

CBS SportsLine.com—Alex Rodriguez
http://www.sportsline.com/u/baseball/mlb/
   players/player_8023.htm

ESPN.com—Alex Rodriguez
http://sports.espn.go.com/mlb/players/
   profile?statsId=5275

MLB.com
http://www.mlb.com

Official Site of the Texas Rangers
http://rangers.mlb.com

Index